HAL•LEONARD®

VIOLIN PLAY-ALONG

 AUDIO ACCESS INCLUDED

SCOTTISH FOLKSONGS

 **PLAYBACK+**
Speed • Pitch • Balance • Loop

CONTENTS

To access audio visit:
www.halleonard.com/mylibrary

Enter Code
8630-1045-1259-2068

ISBN 978-1-4950-3000-0

HAL•LEONARD®
CORPORATION
7777 W. BLUEMOUND RD. P.O. BOX 13819 MILWAUKEE, WI 53213

In Australia Contact:
Hal Leonard Australia Pty. Ltd.
4 Lentara Court
Cheltenham, Victoria, 3192 Australia
Email: ausadmin@halleonard.com.au

Visit Hal Leonard Online at
www.halleonard.com

Jon Vriesacker, violin
Audio arrangements by Peter Deneff
Produced and Recorded by Jake Johnson at Paradyme Productions

Barbara Allen

Traditional English

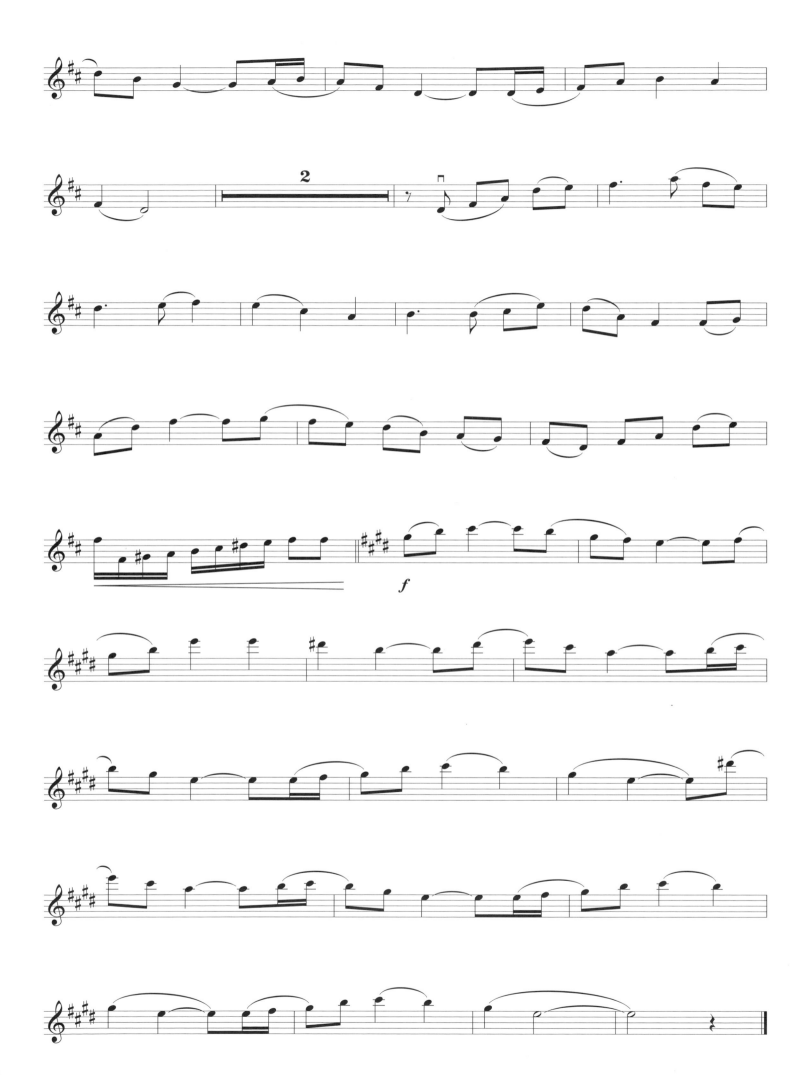

The Blue Bells of Scotland

Words and Music attributed to Mrs. Jordon

Water Is Wide

Traditional

Flow Gently, Sweet Afton

Lyrics by Robert Burns
Music by Alexander Hume

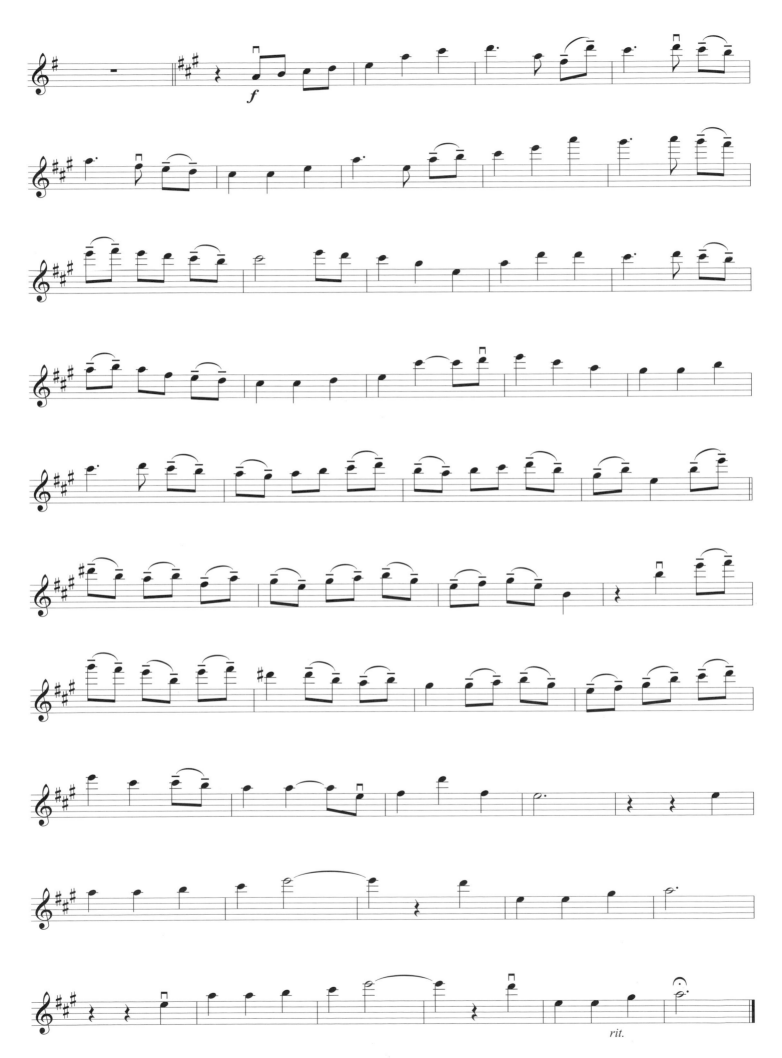

Loch Lomond

Scottish Folksong

The Skye Boat Song

from OUTLANDER (Main Title Theme)

Traditional

Weaving Lilt

Scottish Work Song

Ye Banks and Braes O' Bonnie Doon

Lyrics by Robert Burns
Melody by Charles Miller

The Violin Play-Along Series

Play your favorite songs quickly and easily!

Just follow the music, listen to the CD or online audio to hear how the violin should sound, and then play along using the separate backing tracks. The audio files are enhanced so you can adjust the recordings to any tempo without changing pitch!

1. Bluegrass
00842152 Book/CD Pack $14.99

2. Popular Songs
00842153 Book/CD Pack $14.99

3. Classical
00842154 Book/CD Pack $14.99

4. Celtic
00842155 Book/CD Pack $14.99

5. Christmas Carols
00842156 Book/Online Audio ..$14.99

6. Holiday Hits
00842157 Book/CD Pack $14.99

7. Jazz
00842196 Book/CD Pack $14.99

8. Country Classics
00842230 Book/CD Pack $12.99

9. Country Hits
00842231 Book/CD Pack $14.99

10. Bluegrass Favorites
00842232 Book/CD Pack $14.99

11. Bluegrass Classics
00842233 Book/CD Pack $14.99

12. Wedding Classics
00842324 Book/CD Pack $14.99

13. Wedding Favorites
00842325 Book/CD Pack $14.99

14. Blues Classics
00842427 Book/CD Pack $14.99

15. Stephane Grappelli
00842428 Book/CD Pack $14.99

16. Folk Songs
00842429 Book/CD Pack $14.99

17. Christmas Favorites
00842478 Book/CD Pack $14.99

18. Fiddle Hymns
00842499 Book/CD Pack $14.99

19. Lennon & McCartney
00842564 Book/CD Pack $14.99

20. Irish Tunes
00842565 Book/CD Pack $14.99

21. Andrew Lloyd Webber
00842566 Book/CD Pack $14.99

22. Broadway Hits
00842567 Book/CD Pack $14.99

23. Pirates of the Caribbean
00842625 Book/CD Pack $14.99

24. Rock Classics
00842640 Book/CD Pack $14.99

25. Classical Masterpieces
00842642 Book/CD Pack $14.99

26. Elementary Classics
00842643 Book/CD Pack $14.99

27. Classical Favorites
00842646 Book/CD Pack $14.99

28. Classical Treasures
00842647 Book/CD Pack $14.99

29. Disney Favorites
00842648 Book/CD Pack $14.99

30. Disney Hits
00842649 Book/CD Pack $14.99

31. Movie Themes
00842706 Book/CD Pack $14.99

32. Favorite Christmas Songs
00102110 Book/CD Pack $14.99

33. Hoedown
00102161 Book/CD Pack $14.99

34. Barn Dance
00102568 Book/CD Pack $14.99

35. Lindsey Stirling
00109715 Book/CD Pack $19.99

36. Hot Jazz
00110373 Book/CD Pack $14.99

37. Taylor Swift
00116361 Book/CD Pack $14.99

38. John Williams
00116367 Book/CD Pack $14.99

39. Italian Songs
00116368 Book/CD Pack $14.99

41. Johann Strauss
00121041 Book/CD Pack $14.99

42. Light Classics
00121935 Book/Online Audio ...$14.99

43. Light Orchestra Pop
00122126 Book/Online Audio ...$14.99

44. French Songs
00122123 Book/Online Audio ...$14.99

45. Lindsey Stirling Hits
00123128 Book/Online Audio ...$19.99

46. Piazzolla Tangos
48022997 Book/Online Audio ...$16.99

47. Light Masterworks
00124149 Book/Online Audio ...$14.99

48. Frozen
00126478 Book/Online Audio ...$14.99

49. Pop/Rock
00130216 Book/Online Audio ...$14.99

50. Songs for Beginners
00131417 Book/Online Audio ...$14.99

51. Chart Hits for Beginners
00131418 Book/Online Audio ...$14.99

53. Rockin' Classics
00148768 Book/Online Audio ...$14.99

54. Scottish Folksongs
00148779 Book/Online Audio ...$14.99

55. Wicked
00148780 Book/Online Audio ...$14.99

56. The Sound of Music
00148782 Book/Online Audio ...$14.99

58. The Piano Guys – Wonders
00151837 Book/Online Audio ...$19.99

Disney characters and artwork © Disney Enterprises, Inc.

Prices, contents, and availability subject to change without notice.

HAL•LEONARD®
CORPORATION
7777 W. BLUEMOUND RD. P.O. BOX 13819 MILWAUKEE, WI 53213

www.halleonard.com

0915